How Swim Faster

By

Julian Bradbrook

1

Books in this series
by Julian Bradbrook

How To Swim Faster

How To Run Faster

How To Cycle Faster

Table of Contents

Introduction 13

Glossary of swimming terms..............................15

Chapter 1 – What speed should you be aiming for? 17

    Triathlon swim times................................17

    Sprint distances...................................17

        50m 18

        100m...18

        200m...18

        400m...18

        800m...18

        1500m (the distance that his closest to a mile, swum in a pool)...............................18

Chapter 2 - Technique for the individual strokes 19

    Breaststroke.......................................20

    Butterfly..23

    Back stroke..26

    Freestyle swimming.................................28

Chapter 3 - Overcoming drag.............................29

    Why is drag such a problem?........................29

    General drill exercise to reduce drag............30

Different strokes for different folks..............32

Chapter 4 - Increasing propulsion.......................35

Rolling your body..35

Your kick efficiency.......................................37

How can you make your kicks more efficient
and get more out of less?...............................38

Point your toes to reduce drag......................39

What about kick speed?................................39

A better catch and pull technique....................40

Step one – first contact................................40

Step two – angling down 41

Step three – catching and pulling.................42

Short or long strokes?..................................43

What should you do with your recovering
hand?..43

Drill to improve catch and pull technique....44

Chapter 5 - Speedwork for swimmers.................47

What is speedwork?.......................................47

Fartlek..48

Interval training...49

Other forms of speedwork for swimming.....50

How often should you include speedwork in
your training?..51

Chapter 6 - Streamlining – making yourself long and lean..51

Chapter 7 - Turning for speed.............................53

  Flip turns step by step.....................................54

    Step one – eyes down..................................54

    Step two – look for the T............................55

    Step three – let your body follow.................55

    Step four – use your arms to scull around....55

    Step five – rotate as you push off.................56

    Step six – ride the push off..........................56

    Do not forget to breathe..............................57

Chapter 8 – Diving in to swim fast.....................59

    How to position yourself for a great dive.....59

    What comes next..59

    Getting your focus right...............................60

    On the starting gun.......................................60

    As you hit the water......................................60

    Kick hard and fast..61

Chapter 9 - Outdoor swimming and open water swimming...63

  Acclimatise gradually.....................................63

  Get into the right frame of mind for outdoor swimming..64

  Swim with safety in mind................................64

7

Increasing your range gradually......................65

The advantages of a bit of blubber.................65

Are you afraid of fish?................................65

Think of the environment..............................65

Chapter 10 - Breathing and Swimming fast.........67

Don't forget to breathe out!.........................67

Try not to lift your head..............................68

Do not rotate too far...................................69

Breathe bilaterally....................................69

Keep your head still in between breaths.......70

Chapter 11 - Is there any point in cross training? 73

What types of training can be helpful for
swimmers?...74

Running...74

Cycling..75

Pilates...75

Dance..76

Football and other team games....................76

The gym...76

How much cross training should your regime
include?...76

The brick – swim/run...................................77

Chapter 12 - The importance of core strength to
swimmers..79

Is gym work enough to build core strength? 80

How can you build up your core stability?...80

Pilates..81

Alexander Technique.......................................81

Yoga...82

Chapter 13 - Nutrition and swimming.................83

Where do you get your fuel from?....................83

Are all carbs created equal?...........................84

How much of your diet should be
carbohydrates?..84

The importance of protein in your quest to swim
fast...85

The importance of fats.....................................85

How can you change your diet without too
much pain?...86

Vitamins and minerals......................................86

Before the swim...87

After the race...87

Water, water everywhere but no a drop to
drink?...88

Chapter 14 - Wearing the right kit.......................91

A close shave?..93

What else do you need?....................................96

Pull paddles...96

Pull buoys..97

Underwater camera..97

Goggles...97

Flippers...98

A good timepiece...98

Waterproof MP3 player..................................98

Nose clip...99

Chapter 15 - Developing the mental toughness needed to swim fast.......................................101

Generally...101

Clear and realistic goal setting.....................101

Making a commitment...................................102

Affirmations 103

Visualisation...103

Training with other people before the race day 103

On the day itself...104

Dealing with nerves – letting the stroke rhythm take you over.....................................104

Keep your eye on your own lane..................105

Think of now, not later or before.................106

Chapter 16 - Swimming injuries and how to avoid them...109

Swimmers shoulder......................................109

Knee injury...111

Lower back injuries.....................................111

Neck injuries...112

Conclusion..113

Introduction

Learning to swim is an important rite of passage for any child. You start by being held tightly by your parents and splashing around, and end up with a confident strong stroke across the pool. Then for some reason, adults and teens drift away from the sport, aside from the occasional beach holiday.

In the Western world, swimming has become something that is no longer a regular part of adult life – until you have your own children and teach them to swim.

Watching elite swimmers is fascinating because they make it look so effortless. They seem to glide through the water in a manner that defies its viscosity.

While you may not be able to achieve Olympic speeds; with some skill, effort and dedication you can become a faster swimmer. Given that swimming is as much about technique as it is about strength, the sport is suitable for people of all levels of fitness. It is not weight bearing, and uses the whole body. The water cushions the effect of the exercise on your joints, meaning that the elderly and those recovering from injuries from other sports can train frequently without damaging their bodies.

So how can this book help you? To begin with, we will look at the speeds that Olympic champions do achieve, by way of inspiration. The book then considers what speeds are more realistic for various levels of amateur swimming. There are four main swimming strokes in the sport: freestyle, butterfly, breaststroke and back stroke.

The fastest is freestyle, and the majority of this book is devoted to that stroke because it is the one in which the fastest speeds are achievable. It is also arguably the easiest. However, there are some tips on how to swim faster using the other strokes too. The book then considers the effect of drag on the body, and breaks down the process of swimming bit by bit so that you can hone your technique, one aspect at a time. By taking every moment of your swimming race bit by bit, we will look at techniques you can adopt and drills that you can do to make you go faster, from the position of your head right down to the angle of your toes.

Advice about nutrition for swimming fast and avoidance of injuries completes the book, so that you can conclude with an holistic approach to learning to swim faster.

"The water is your friend. You don't have to fight with water, just share the same spirit as the water, and it will help you move." Aleksandr Popov

Glossary of swimming terms

Backstroke – a stroke that is used when the swimmer lies on his back
Bilateral breathing – breathing on both sides
Breaststroke – the swimmer uses a frog like kick and a simultaneous sculling like motion with the arms and hands
Brick – a training workout comprising two disciplines (for example a swim run workout)
Butterfly – a swim stroke that has the swimmer looking like a butterfly, with arms and legs moving simultaneously
Catch – the part of a swimming stroke that involves the initial contact of the arm with the water, as you "catch" it
Crossover –what happens when your arm crosses over the front of your head in freestyle, when it should always be level with the shoulder
Drag – the effect of the friction of the water on your body, which slows down a swimmer
Drill – a training exercise that focuses on a particular skill
Fartlek – literal translation is speed play, a fun way to practise swimming faster
Intervals – a method of speed training
Lift – the force that controls a swimmer's movement up and down

Nose clip – a funny looking piece of plastic to keep water from going up your nose

Flip turn – the somersault like turn that swimmers perform at the end of the pool

Flippers – a bit like paddles pulls, but these are the bigger ones that are floppier as they emulate the action of fins.

Pull – the moment when the hands first make contact with the water in a swimming stroke

Pull buoy – a floatation aid that you typically put between your legs, so that you can isolation your arm action to work on in swimming drills.

Pull paddles – usually plastic, these are objects that are fitted onto your hands in training to increase the surface area available for catching as much water as possible.

Propulsion – the act of propelling your body forward

Scissor kicking – similar to crossover but for legs

Speedwork – training that is specifically targeting your speed

Streamline – the part of a stroke or push off from a dive or turn where the swimmer is stretched out into a streamline position.

Chapter 1 – What speed should you be aiming for?

The speed that you are aiming for depends on your overall level of fitness, the time you have available for training and the amount of effort that you are prepared to put in.

Triathlon swim times

The distance for the swim leg of a standard Olympic triathlons is 0.9 miles. Given that triathletes have an ordeal ahead of them being a long run and a longish cycle, they do not typically give the swimming leg of the triathlon their full energy levels. Triathletes may not use their legs as much as other swimmers, given that they have many more miles to cover. Triathletes should be aiming to swim their outdoor mile in under 30 minutes.

Sprint distances

In racing conditions, swim sprinters are drug tested, and their times are measured with specially calibrated timepieces. This may seem over the top for the enthusiastic amateur, but if you were to compete against elite athletes, you should bear in mind that world records are the following times:

50m
Men – 20:91 Cesar Cielo from Brazil
Women – 23:73 Britta Steffen from Germany

100m
Men – 46:91 Cesar Cielo from Brazil
Women – 52:07 Britta Steffen from Germany

200m
Men – 1:42:00 Paul Biedermann from Germany
Women – 1:52:48 Frederica Pellegrini from Italy

400m
Men – 3:40:07 Paul Biedermann from Germany
Women – 3:59:15 Frederica Pellegrini from Italy

800m
Men – 7:32:12 Zhang Lin from China
Women – 8:14:10 Rebecca Adlington from the United Kingdom

1500m (the distance that his closest to a mile, swum in a pool)
Men – 14:31:02 Sun Yang from China
Women – 15:42:54 Kate Ziegler from the United States

For an amateur athlete, if you multiply those champions' times by 1.5, you should get a time that is achievable after considerable practise.

Chapter 2 - Technique for the individual strokes

There are a number of different swimming strokes that you can try. Most people start off with "doggy paddle" when they are learning to swim. By "bicycling" the arms, wrists and hands, you make steady progress is made through the water. It is an easy stroke to explain to children, and is the natural progression from treading water, which is where those who are new to the swimming pool should start. Learning to tread water first is important from a safety point of view, and also to give a new swimmer some confidence that they are in charge of their own pace.

But swimmers do not make much progress with doggy paddle. The purpose of this stroke is really a learning one.

As a new swimmer is more confident and becomes stronger, they will want to progress to the front crawl, breast stroke or the butterfly. Techniques for swimming fast using these will be explained shortly, but the breast stroke is considered the easiest because it is the gentlest and can be done as slowly as you like, to begin with. Beginners can also do breast stroke without putting their heads in the water. As we will learn later, lifting your head causes unnecessary drag and slows you down, but someone who is afraid of water might like to bring their confidence up with breast stroke.

The next easiest stroke is the front crawl, where the kick feels natural and your arms move alternately in front of you to move through the water. The butterfly stroke, on the other hand, is so difficult that it is a significant achievement to be able to do it at all, let alone to do it quickly! However, if you swim competitively you will probably come across this stroke in relays. It is a technical achievement to be able to pull off a decent butterfly stroke, and many swimmers include it in their regime to showcase their technical skill.

Most of the advice in this book contained in this book is aimed at freestyle (front crawl) swimmers, because this is the most common. But there follows some advice about the other strokes, because you may wish to hone the techniques necessary to increase your speed using those.

Breaststroke

Despite its name, breaststroke places lots more emphasis on the swimmer's legs and the kick than freestyle. The majority of the breaststroke swimmer's propulsion may come from the arms, but a swimmer's legs do their fair share of the work too.

Accordingly, it is important to do plenty of strength exercises, particularly ones that focus on your thighs, to try to get powerful legs. You can use cross training workouts in the gym to build stronger quad, adductors and abductors. Start with small weights and gradually build up to larger ones in small stages, to avoid injury.

When performing your "frog kick" in the pool, make sure you control the whole of the kick carefully. Sometimes it can be tempting to focus on the push out, and let your legs drift back together to start a new kick. By letting the momentum of the kick control you, rather than the other way around, you lose efficiency. To get the best performance out of your legs while frog kicking, it is best to bring your heels together decisively to set your legs into the optimum position.

When it comes to your arms, there are three phases in breaststroke. The first is the outsweep, where your arms sweep out from a streamlined position. At this point, you need to make sure that your palms are facing outwards rather than downwards (as they do with freestyle). If you do most of your training with freestyle, you may find this difficult! After the insweep, where you press the water around you to the sides in a semi-circle to the side of your body, the next stage is the recover. In this phase, make sure that your recovery involves shooting your hands forward with some force, rather than pushing them gently.

There are a number of drills which you can do to improve and quicken your breaststroke, which typically involve isolating one stage of the breaststroke so that you can perfect it:

- Streamline kicking – by stretching out your arms in front of you, propel yourself across the pool using your legs only. This makes you focus on making your frog kicks more powerful, but it also means that you must try to be as streamlined as possible with your core, torso and arms.
- Do a couple of lengths of breast stroke arms, but with your legs doing flutter kicks. This means that you can concentrate on getting the power you need into your arms, without having to worry about getting the timing right with your breaststroke arms and legs (which some swimmers find the most challenging part of this stroke). Focus on every stage of the three part arm action and make sure that you are doing it to the best of your ability.
- Kicking on your back – by floating on your back, you do not need to use your arms for any other reason but to steer yourself and keep stable. Now propel yourself across the pool using your breaststroke kick. What is the point of doing this on your back? This way, you can concentrate on keeping your knees below your waist. This, as you will see from chapter 3 below, is crucial to minimising drag.
- Do a couple of lengths using only your fists. This will feel bizarre if you have never tried it before. But if you do a couple

of lengths of the pool using only your fists, you will concentrate on the strength of your arms, rather than the cupping of your hands. Do not worry about the indelicate nature of your style at this point. Using your fists to propel you across the water will enable you to think about the brute force at your disposal.

- Finally, swim a couple of lengths concentrating on how your head is behaving. Lifting your head too far out of the water is detrimental to the drag that you cause, so this is an important thing to master. By imagining that there is a ceiling above your head that you will crash into should you bob up too high, you can maintain a disciplined approach to coming up for air.

Butterfly

The thing about the butterfly stroke is that it is impossible to do it badly. As an advanced technique, you can either do it well, or not do it at all. The stroke was first "invented" in the 1930s, and is typically something that has to be taught rather than copied from other swimmers. The stroke evolved from breaststroke, and was developed by some swimmers who were experimenting with their arm techniques. Who knows, maybe you will come up with a stroke of your own while you are following this book!

Doing the butterfly stroke incorrectly risks shoulder injury, because it places more stress than other strokes on this part of your body.

The stroke gets its name from the simultaneous movement of the arms, which resemble wings as they cut through the water. The "pulling" stage is faster than that of freestyle, but the overall speeds reached in butterfly are not as quick, because the recovery time needed between strokes is longer. To do the butterfly, a swimmer pushes his arms out into the glide position, which is similar to the beginning of the breaststroke. But instead of pulling back through the water in a sculling motion, they are pulled down through to one third of the way towards the hips, raised and butterflied through the air to start again.

Butterfly used to be swum with breaststroke (frog) legs, but within the last few decades the stroke changed to the dolphin kick, which is more like freestyle kicking, but instead of kicking independently, the legs move together. This action creates a wave of activity along the body, and is fascinating to watch.

Breathing in butterfly is difficult to time, as there is only one window in the stroke when the swimmer can take the chance (when their head pops out of the water just before recovery). Most swimmers breathe once every two strokes, but certain elite swimmers will breathe on every stroke. This is only possible with a sophisticated technique.

Swimming drills that can make you go faster doing butterfly stroke include:

- Swimming as far as you can underwater. Obviously you will not be doing the arms of the butterfly stroke, but by practising your dolphin kick underwater you can perfect the technique whilst minimising drag. Some swimmers like to use fins in the first instance, but after a few lengths without them you should become proficient at a flutter kick underwater, so that the next time you go back to "normal" butterfly you can steam across the pool!

- Check your arm positions on dry land. By running through the stroke on dry land, you or the training partner who is spotting you can make sure that you are lifting your head during the press section of the stroke, and thereby planning your breathing in the right moment. Do not feel stupid running through strokes on dry land (although it may feel odd when you first try). It is good enough for Olympic athletes!

- Do not be tempted to train with a float between your legs for the butterfly stroke, because this will put your legs in the wrong position in relation to your body and "teach" you the wrong positioning for your arms.

Back stroke

Back stroke can be compared with upside down freestyle. It is the only racing style that allows a slightly different start to the others, because diving forwards and turning would be too awkward and diving in backwards would be downright dangerous.

The kick that is used is the same as in freestyle, so the same caveats apply. Your legs should not drop too far below the water, but neither should they come up very high, in case you create too much drag.

For your arms, you need to beware of thrashing your whole body from side to side. This is a common problem with backstroke. Thrashing is not helpful because not only does it waste energy, the sharp movements of the head and neck means that you run the risk of injury.

A further potential problem is that by definition back stroke swimmers cannot see where they are going. Instead, swimmers who use backstroke will have to learn to use markers on the sides of the pool, and also on the ceiling depending on how well equipped your pool is.

There are various drills that you can do to improve your back stroke speed:

- The streamline kick drill involves stretching your arms above your head, and holding your hands together. This isolates the legs, and allows the swimmer to concentrate on their kicking. Focus at this point on keeping your hips low, and minimising the splashing that occurs when you kick.

- The cup drill. It is important for a swimmer to keep a steady head in more ways than one! By half filling a plastic cup with water and placing it on the swimmer's forehead, make sure that their head does not turn from side to side while they are swimming along. See how long your training partner can keep the cup full of water without losing it into the pool! This is a fun way of driving home the message that moving your head from side to side is a waste of energy. It also shows the swimmer that what you do to the whole of your body affects the position of your head – by kicking too vigorously, you can upset the cup, which means that your kicking technique is too violent.

- One arm at a time drill. Once again, this drill helps to keep the head steady. But the main aim of the drill is to encourage mindfulness from the point of view of the swimmer in relation to their arm actions. So if you want to try out this drill, swim first using normal kicks, but only your right arm. Then swim back using only your left arm. Place the resting arm loosely at your side. This exercise encourages should control, because you will need to take great care when doing this exercise.

- The thumbs up drill. Swimmers often perform drills that will make them stronger, or focus on the shoulder action. But this drill focuses on the way in which your hand will enter the water. When you are swimming on your back, lift your lead arm out of the water thumb first. When that arm is at ninety degrees to your body, rotate the hand until your little finger is positioned to hit the water first, to make your catch.

Freestyle swimming

With every sport, fashions come and go about what coaches advise. With freestyle (often called front crawl), twenty years ago you would have heard coaches advising their charges to adopt an "S" pattern in the pull phase of their arm stroke. The theory went that by covering more distance underwater by making the shape of the letter "S", the swimmer has more chance to catch more water. However, recent practice is to take a more streamlined approach. The tips and techniques set out in chapter 4 below deal specifically with methods of improving your freestyle times.

Chapter 3 - Overcoming drag

According to champion swimmers, overcoming drag is the single most important thing that you can do to make yourself swim faster. The rules of most competitions prevent swimmers from doing what would be the most effective thing to do this – swimming underwater. But you will see from this chapter that many of the techniques elite swimmers employ to overcome drag involve keeping most of their bodies beneath the surface. To those who think that swimming faster is simply about swimming harder, it can seem odd that basic physics is really the answer. Someone with a large aerobic capacity can, with poor drag resistance, be beaten in a swimming race by a couch potato who has mastered drag resistance. This may seem unfair, but it is worth remembering.

Why is drag such a problem?

The typical swimmer's position is that their lower body is positioned much deeper in the water than their arms, shoulders and head. The body forms a diagonal line, slanting downwards from the head to the feet. People who are learning to swim tend to swim at a steeper angle than experienced swimmers, because they are tempted to assume the position of treading water and may be unsettled by floating horizontally.

This diagonal position is sometimes known as the "swimming uphill" position, where every part of the body down from the chest to the feet creates drag. If you think that the effect of drag is being overstated, consider that Olympic swimmers and even amateurs who take the sport seriously shave their body hair to eliminate as much drag as possible.

This may seem dramatic to someone who has only just started the sport. However, having the mental picture of your body positioned in the swimming uphill position as you are moving through the water means that you can visualise what you need to do to improve the profile that you present as you swim. Anything that you do to improve that profile and become more horizontal will reduce the drag you cause.

General drill exercise to reduce drag

Firstly swim through the water for two lengths thinking carefully about the profile that you are offering. Feel the water resistance on your chest, legs and hips. Where does it feel the most profound?

Next, swim for two lengths focusing on each of the following body parts (mentioned below) at a time (so two lengths with the head, then the lead arm and so on). Think about each part and how you can improve its resistance profile.

Head

The more you raise your head, the more your legs and hips will fall further down into the pool. This is because your body is a bit like a see saw. If you lift one part, another will drop further into the water.

On the two lengths of this exercise when you are particularly concentrating on the position of your head, you may notice that whenever you lift your head to look forward to see where you are, your feet sink a bit.

Given that the most effective shape for reducing drag is a stretched out body that is evenly horizontal, it makes sense to lower your head to the water at all times. If you can control your breathing well enough, put your head under the water and only take breathes when you need to. You should notice during the course of these two lengths that are focusing on the head that the drag is better when your head is underwater.

Lead arm

When it comes to arms, you should do your swimming in the water, as opposed to on it. This means that when you reach your arm forward, it should be plunged deep into the water, rather than raised high and stretched forward. You need to limit the distance that you lift your arm at this point. Not only does this result in a better drag profile, but it is more energy efficient.

Any reduction in the effort that you need to put into the stroke is helpful because it leaves more "in the tank" for later. Furthermore, the deeper you manage to get your arms, the lower you will pull the front of your body and the better profile you will present to the water for the purposes of drag resistance.

Chest

Given that your lungs are full of air, their natural tendency is to float. Accordingly, you need to bear this in mind when you consider how you approach the water. Try to press your chest into the pool and keep on doing so as you move along, to recalibrate your position.

It can be tempting as you take deep breaths to lift your chest out of the water as well as your head. However, this temptation should be resisted as it can disturb your drag profile.

Different strokes for different folks

There is no "one size fits all" approach to swimming and positioning. Some people (particularly if they are new to the sport) may find it difficult to change from the "uphill" position due to a lack of confidence. The uphill position at least feels safe, especially if you pop your head up to look around and convince yourself that you are still safe and floating.

But there is also the issue of body type to take into account. Surprisingly, those with more body fat on their legs and bottoms may float more easily than people with less fat and more muscle. This is because muscle and bone are more dense than fat.

So does that mean that a couch potato will find it easier to swim more aerodynamically? Not really, because you need to be toned and strong to keep making slight adjustments to your position to keep drag to a minimum. Swimming fast is not a competition to see who floats the easiest – it is about whose profile is the best for moving through the water the fastest. This is largely a matter of trial and error, and every so often in your training regime you should return to the exercise above where you go through each part of your body in turn and consider its drag profile.

Chapter 4 - Increasing propulsion

Now that you have reduced the drag that your body creates in the water, it is time to increase propulsion. That is to say, the power with which you propel yourself forward needs to be increased. There are a number of different ways in which you can do this. Some techniques involve using your whole body, and others focus on enhancing the power of your legs and your arms.

Water is 1,000 times more viscose than air, which means that you need to apply much more force to make progress through it than your cycling or running colleagues do to propel themselves through the air.

What follows in this chapter are tips that are specifically designed for freestyle.

Rolling your body

This may seem weird when you first start to do it, but rolling your body is an important way of increasing your propulsion. This is because it allows you to unharness the energy that your large and powerful back muscles are capable of producing. The muscles in your back are often neglected – not least because you cannot see them – but when they are partnered with your shoulder muscles, you can get the best propulsion available from your upper body.

Some swimmers claim that rolling is a consequence of rather than a cause of swimming fast. They claim that they roll only because of the momentum that they have built up by getting into a strong stroke rhythm. Others disagree, taking the view that making a conscious effort to roll yourself slightly from the hips with each stroke means that you will be able to drive yourself forward. Swimmers should roll on an imaginary central axis, going from their head to their toes. Rolling on any other axis means that you are at risk from causing your arms to cross over, which wastes energy and puts you at risk of injury. Crossing over can also be a sign that you are having difficulty timing your breathing.

You should not roll to more than 45 degrees when swimming fast. When you first try to roll, you may not feel comfortable rolling at an angle of more than 30 degrees. If you have never tried rolling as a technique before, start gentle and work your way up to something more definite. However, if you go beyond 45 degrees you end up compromising your own stability.

Once you have become used to this technique, you will notice a change and an increase in your endurance. This is because your swimming technique will be more efficient, so you will be able to swim for longer without getting tired.

Your kick efficiency

Professional swimmers tend to have a triangular body shape, where the top half of their bodies are stronger and wider than the bottom half. Elite swimmers have powerful looking shoulders and arms, and narrow slim waists. Their legs also seem strong and muscular.

But when scientists have analysed the relative contributions of each part of a swimmer's body to a swimmer's progress, it seems that the percentage of propulsion derived from the legs is only between 10 and 15%. This seems surprising given the overall size of the leg muscles, and may seem strange to triathletes, whose other two sports are all about the legs!

This does put swimming propulsion into perspective, and give you some idea about where your efforts should really be focussed. Until you heard the results of the research above, did you assume that the arms and legs contributed a bit more evenly, in the region of, say, 60:40% to overall propulsion efforts?

So if kicking is not about propulsion, why do swimmers bother? The answer is not simple, thanks to the complexity of fluid mechanics. When swimmers kick, they exercise a stabilising force that enables the rest of the stroke to be so effective. So kicking is a supportive rather than a dominant process, but important nonetheless in the wider enterprise of trying to swim fast. And in addition to being solely about balance, kicking continues forward momentum during the recovery phase of an arm stroke (whichever stroke you have chosen). Finally, your legs can also help with the positioning of your upper body, thanks to the see saw effect mentioned above.

How can you make your kicks more efficient and get more out of less?

First, try to straighten your legs. If you are new to the sport, you are probably kicking from the knee as this seems to create the most turbulence at the back and seems to have the biggest dramatic effect!

Some swimming coaches encourage their swimmers to kick from the hip, which sounds strange until you try it. Kicking from the hip means than you are less likely to make your feet pop up from the water, meaning that your kick will have a lower drag profile.

You can bend your knee slightly while kicking, but not significantly, because bending your knee a lot means that you are neglecting your upper leg muscles which are the ones with the real power to propel you forward.

Next, stop scissor kicking. Scissor kicks happen when you open your legs too wide and kick horizontally as well as vertically, and end up looking like a pair of scissors! This can be something that you do naturally without realising it, and is often an instinctive response to feeling unstable. However, scissor kicking creates lots of drag and as such needs to be drilled out of you!

Point your toes to reduce drag

There is so much to remember when you are swimming. But if you can remember to get into the habit of pointing your toes, it is worth doing so for two reasons. Firstly, pointing your toes reduces the drag you cause, because it presents a better profile than a flat foot. But secondly and perhaps more importantly, flat feet create negative propulsion. In other words, having flat feet can mean that you push water towards you rather than away from you, which propels you in the opposite direction. So failing to point your toes means that you are actually working against yourself!

What about kick speed?

For triathletes who have a long run and cycle ahead of them after their swim, efficiency is as important as speed, due to the need to conserve energy. Triathletes still want to go fast, but not if it costs too much in terms of their long term efficiency. So for them, a 2 beat kick is ideal. This means that for every stroke set, they have 2 kicks. Not only is this efficient at conserving energy, it also has an adequate stabilising effect.

Before they address their minds to the issue in a drill, most swimmers adopt a 4 beat kick, which means 4 kicks for every stroke set. If this sounds familiar, it may be what comes naturally for you, and is by no means wrong. 2 beat kicks are better, but if you are kicking with pointed toes and relatively straight legs, there is no hurry or imperative to change to a 2 beat method. Swimmers who are shorter in stature (or tall swimmers with short legs) may find that it is just too slow.

A better catch and pull technique

Have you been pounding away at the pool for weeks on end without much to show for it? This can be a problem if you subscribe to the idea that the way to get better results is to put more time into your training endeavour, even if that training is no different from what you have been doing before.

If you haven't been working on your catch and pull technique, then just a couple of sessions of focussing on this will stand you in good stead and improve your power, and therefore your speed. Catch and pull theory is something that tends to evolve every few years. A while ago having an "S" shaped pull seemed to be the most recommended method, but this has been discredited. So what is the best way to catch and pull with your arms?

Step one – first contact

As we have learnt above, it is important to point your toes when kicking. However, given that proportionately so much more power comes from your arms, it is doubly important to point your fingers when you are reaching forward for the first part of the catch. Your fingers should be stretched out, as though they are reaching towards the far end of the pool. At this point take care to ensure that you are not crossing over, which means that your lead arm is venturing into the other arm's side of the water.

At this stage of the stroke, your arm should be two thirds extended. Your hand should be cupped, but in a relatively shallow way. Your hands should not, for example, be making a 90 degree angle at your knuckles.

Step two – angling down

You will have read above that you should be kicking from the hip in order to get the most out of your leg power. The same principle applies to getting the most out of your hands. When it comes to extending your lead arm into the water, you need to be angling your fingers down through the water at your wrist, rather than at your knuckles. For the same reasons that flat feet are a bad idea (because they push water in the wrong direction), clawed hands can increase drag and make you go slower.

Throughout the stroke, it is important to hold your fingers loosely together. In the excitement of a race or the nervousness of a triathlon swim, you might tense up and clench them together without realising that you are doing this. Try to resist this behaviour, because for a perfect stroke your palm should be parallel with the bottom of the pool.

Step three – catching and pulling

When you have got your hand into a good position, the most simple way to remember what should happen next is that you need to be pressing, not pushing the water behind you.

It is often said that elite athletes glide through the water rather than thrash their way through it. This is because they are pressing, not pushing. When you have pressed the water to the 6 o'clock position (where your arm is directly below your body), then your palm should change from facing the bottom of the pool to facing the side of the pool that you are leaving behind you until you are ready to take it out of the water and it becomes the recovery arm, while the other arm leads. At this stage, your arm should be fully extended downwards.

It is tempting to think that the harder you pull, the faster you will go. Counter-intuitive as it seems, this is not true because you will not be able to harness all of the energy you use, which makes the process inefficient.

Instead, try to press firmly without sculling. Swimming coaches used to teach that an "S" shape was the best way to extract the most power from the pull section of swimming. But scientists and coaches have now realised that this is also a waste of energy and even worse, a bigger injury risk for swimmers than a straighter pull.

Short or long strokes?

Short strokes are inevitable for people with limited mobility, and are recommended for sprinters. However, for endurance swimmers (and triathletes can include themselves in this group given the nature of their whole event), longer strokes are preferable. Elite athletes typically do longer strokes when they are training, and shorter ones in races.

What should you do with your recovering hand?

The recovering hand is the one that is not the lead hand. So at the time when the lead arm is doing the "catch and pull" action, the recovering hand should be positioning itself to start another stroke. So when the lead arm is perpendicular to your body underwater, the recovering hand is just above your head.

The key to a swift and smooth recovery is to keep your elbow high. But do not be tempted to recover your arm from the water too soon, and do not be tempted to recover your arm when it is fully extended. Bend it slightly by lifting your elbow, and make sure that the recovering hand is controlled and smooth in its movement out of the water and into readiness for the next stroke.

Drill to improve catch and pull technique
Land drill

One of the best ways to improve your catch and pull technique is ironically to do some practice on dry land. If you do not have access to a waterproof camera, it can be helpful to record your natural stroke technique on dry land with a regular camera, before applying the points made above so that you can make some alterations. Then make another recording, and study how fluid the movement has become. Of course, the proof of the pudding is in the eating as the whole point of the catch and pull technique is to combat the viscosity of water. Accordingly, once you have done some land drills and you get back into the pool, you should notice the difference straightaway as you develop the ability to press water rather than push it.

Using pull paddles

Another method of improving your catch and pull technique is to use pull paddles. These are strange looking things that resemble flippers, which fit onto your hands with straps. They increase the resistance you face when pulling through the water, because of their large surface area. The theory goes that when you remove the paddles, swimming normally becomes easier because you are so much stronger. However, pull paddles can cause problems if you are not used to using them, because you are subjecting your body to a greater strain, and therefore a greater chance of injury.

To mitigate these risks, make sure that you have read the instructions on the pull paddles, have chosen an appropriate size for you and that you warm up and cool down adequately.

Chapter 5 - Speedwork for swimmers

Does the expression "speedwork" fill you full of dread or excitement? Or indifference? Speedwork is something that swimming teachers and coaches love because it spices up lessons and delivers fast results. However, if you are training on your own without outside help, speedwork can be neglectedor overlooked.

What is speedwork?

There are many forms of speedwork, but generally the term means exercises that are designed to increase your speed by focusing your efforts on particular activities. Some swimmers do speedwork without realising it, whilst others make it part of their targeted workout goals.

[If you are training in a pool, much of your speed is governed by the efficiency of your turns] and how powerful your dives are. Improving these two features is covered further down the book. This chapter focuses on the different methods you could use to improve your speed when you are already swimming in one direction.

There are two main forms of speedwork in swimming training, although individual coaches are always trying to devise new ways to get their swimming students interested in trying different drills.

Fartlek

Speedwork can be formal or informal. Informal techniques include fartlek, which is typically associated with running, but can be applied to any sport that means you to make progress over distance like cycling, swimming, canoeing or rowing.

The word itself is a Swedish one, and means "speed play", so you can already tell from the "play" part that it is meant to be fun and informal. The system originated from the coach for the Swedish cross country team. Irritated by being beaten by the Finns, the Swedish coach devised a system that enabled his team to get faster at running, without getting exhausted or fed up with the sport. The coach did not approve of putting unnecessary or unrealistic pressure on his team. Instead, he thought that an approach that put the fun back into sport would get more buy-in and therefore more effort from his team.

Fartlek simply involves doing short bursts of speedy swimming, interspersed with slower, more gentle strokes. So if you apply fartlek to your training in a swimming pool, you could do one gentle length, followed by a sprint, followed by a length of backstroke, and so on.

Or you could make it even more informal by switching halfway across the pool from gentle to sprint. The point of fartlek is to make your reaction times quicker, and get your body used to switching between different speeds, so that when the moment

comes in a race when you need to switch into top gear, your body is comfortable doing so.⌋
Fartlek is a type of speedwork that you can do alone, or with other swimmers. You can squeeze a few minutes onto the end of your workout or devote half an hour to it. The beauty of fartlek is its informality. Once you have seen the benefits that fartlek can bring, you may be tempted to formalise your speedwork and try some interval training.

Interval training

On the face of it, interval training seems a little like fartlek, but is more formal. So as its name suggests⌊interval training involves changing the speed at which you swim in predefined chunks of time or distance.⌋

As with other types of interval training for various sports, the intense bursts of energy used in the sprint stages means that your body is exercising anaerobically. That is to say that the body does not have time to use oxygen in the process of burning energy. This anaerobic process causes a build-up of lactic acid, which can be difficult for your body to get rid of.

Regular interval training improves your body's efficiency at processing lactic acid, and therefore improves your ability to cope with the high energy sprints that are needed to race at high speeds. The periods of slower swimming that follows the burst of intensity offer your body the chance it needs to take to recover.

The exact pattern of your interval training depends on where you are in your journey to becoming a faster swimmer. A complete beginner may feel that one length at sprinting speed is enough, whereas a seasoned swimmer may have to do at least three lengths at sprint speed before they feel the benefit. With all types of training it is important to warm up and cool down, but this is particularly true of interval training, because the periods of intensity put immense pressure on your muscles. After a session of interval training, make sure that you do at least four lengths of gentle swimming in any stroke, to allow your muscles the opportunity to elongate again and begin recovery.

Other forms of speedwork for swimming

One of the most powerful methods of speedwork is actually entering races. It is one thing to time yourself in the pool on your own, and quite another to feel the adrenalin racing through your body as you try to beat your opponent. Participating in races can be the most effective form of speedwork there is sometimes you need an opponent to pull against to achieve your best speed.

How often should you include speedwork in your training?

If you are serious about training, speedwork should feature twice a week in your regime. It does not have to take up the whole of your training session. You will see a benefit after two sessions of just fifteen minutes a week. If you do it too often, it will take over your training and distract you from the other things that your swimming training is trying to achieve, like improving technique and building strength. However, if you do it too infrequently, speedwork will feel too hard, and you will not get the benefit of the intense bursts of energy.

It is important to keep recording your times, so that you can track your progress and work out whether your speedwork is having the desired effects. It is best to write this down, so that you can reflect on the general pattern of your times over the previous six months.

Chapter 6 - Streamlining – making yourself long and lean

It may be particularly galling, but the fastest times that you will travel in the pool when swimming are the moments when you enter the water from a diver, or when you push off the wall from a turn. There is no way that you can generate the same level of propulsion from your arms and legs.

So whilst this is not, strictly speaking, connected to swimming fast through strokes, harnessing the power of these steam line moments is important to get your times down for races and for general swimming.

How can you do this? The answer is that you need to make your body long and lean to present the most drag friendly profile to the water.

Making yourself long simply involves stretching your fingers, hands and arms as far in front of your as possible, with your arms tucked neatly and smoothly against your ears. Likewise, your legs should be pressed together, with toes pointed and ankles resting against one another.

The core of your body should be tight (holding your tummy in!). Your buttocks should be clenched but not uncomfortably so.

Making yourself streamlined is a skill that can be enhanced by dry land training, so that your coach or a friend can tell you whether your profile is indeed as sleek as it can be.

But streamlining will also be helped by the types of cross training activities that enhance muscle condition, like Pilates, yoga and working out in the gym.

Chapter 7 - Turning for speed

If you have spent hours perfecting the art of
swimming fast laps, it would be a shame to let
yourself down by performing slow or cumbersome
turns when you reach the edge of the pool.
By turning properly in the pool, you can reduce the
amount of momentum that is lost, and keep up
your stroke rhythm. You can also take the
opportunity to kick off properly from the side of
the pool, so that you can use the power of your leg
muscles and give your arms a few seconds' rest.
If you are a triathlete, you may be forgiven for
wondering why you should bother learning how to
do a flip turn. After all, you will not be turning on
anything in the sea, river or lake where your swim
leg will take place! But perfecting this manoeuvre
will mean that your training sessions can be a lot
more effective, and that you can therefore get your
speed up, which will pay off when you are
swimming in open water. It also means that you
will have to learn to swim uninterrupted. Even
pausing for a split second at the side of the pool
interrupts your flow enough to mean that
swimming in open water without these mini pauses
becomes much harder.
If you are a sprint swimmer, there is even more
reason as to why you need to learn to turn and dive
(in a later chapter) for speed. If your sprint
distance is 200m, for example, and you consider

that dives and turns constitute around 50m of that 200m in total, then your diving and turning is nearly a quarter of your total race distance. Yet does diving and turning constitute a quarter of your training focus?

There is quite a learning curve involved when you are teaching yourself to flip turn, but like every new skill it simply requires practice.

Flip turns step by step

If you have never tried this before, it is the weirdness of the sensation that makes it seem so difficult. Human beings were not designed to swim around almost in circles, so do not be surprised that it feels strange. Do not expect to be able to try this in one go. You may even find that you can only make it to one stage at a time, but that is fine as long as you get to the end eventually!

Step one – eyes down

The first step in learning a flip turn is learning to measure and gauge where you are in the pool with reference to looking at the floor, as opposed to looking at the pool side. The bottom of the pool, as you will have discovered from the above chapter about reducing drag, should be where you are looking anyway. If you are not focused on the floor, and "pop up" from time to time to see how far away the edge of the pool really is, not only will you have interrupted your stroke rhythm, you will also have disrupted your drag resistance efforts.

Step two – look for the T

When you have become used to following the black lines along the floor of the pool for navigation, you will notice that there is a black T at the end of the line, to signify that the edge of the pool is around two feet away.

As your forehead reaches the T, tuck your head into your body and pull hard with you lead arm in the water, using your legs to kick gently and allow yourself to swim downward.

Step three – let your body follow

If you have not done a somersault since primary school, this may feel rather strange, particularly as your last somersault would have been on dry land. However, do not forget that a somersault style action is what you need to make a successful turn. Let your body go up and over to follow your head. Do not give in to the instinct that tells you to float and swim around horizontally in a circle (this sounds very strange but will make sense the next time that you are in the pool).

Step four – use your arms to scull around

Your bottom is in the air and your head is right down. How do you complete the somersault? The answer is that you have to use your arms at this point, as your legs are unlikely to be able to create

the propulsion in the right direction to pull you
around far enough.

Step five – rotate as you push off
As you push off the wall, your legs will resemble
the position they might be in if you were sitting on
a chair on the side of the pool. It is important at
this point to push off the wall as hard as you can
with your feet. However, you need to bear in mind
that unless you rotate your body, your face will be
facing the ceiling, as opposed to the floor.
This rotation should not be a jerky movement.
Instead, it should be a gentle twist that gets you
where you want to be at the end of the manoeuvre.

Step six – ride the push off
The momentum that the push off the wall should
give you is best ridden if you stretch up your arms
above your head, tucked in close by your ears.
This means that you are presenting the profile to
the water that will cause the least drag, and enable
you to get the most out of the power you put into
the push off.
Do not leave it too long before you take a stroke to
restart the swimming. Too often beginners can wait
for the push off to run out of steam so that they
slow down and need to speed up again. This is a
waste of energy. Start your first stroke before the
speed generated by the push off slows down.
Again, this is something that you need to practice
to be able to judge. When you start flip turning,

you will no doubt do a few turns which result in running out of steam too soon, but that is absolutely fine in training. At this point, you should just be proud of yourself for having mastered the flip turn and a little smug compared to those who are still grabbing the side of the pool and pushing off!

Do not forget to breathe
This may sound like unnecessary advice. But forgetting to control your breathing is a more accurate description of why some attempts at flip turning can be too frightening for the swimmer to continue. If you are not careful you can end up swallowing water as you come to the second half of the somersault. This is unnerving. To avoid this, exhale slowly throughout the procedure. Not only does this prevent you from inhaling water, this will also relax you as you work your way around.

Chapter 8 – Diving in to swim fast

Diving is a discipline in itself. Diving for competitions is beyond the scope of this book, but the principles of a streamlined end to a dive are similar whether you are making a performance dive or starting a swimming race.

In a performance dive, you enter the water vertically and give no thought to your next stroke or how you will move away from the action. It does not matter if you swim leisurely to the side after you have emerged from the deep water. One a speed dive however, the whole point of the action is to work your way best into your stroke.

How to position yourself for a great dive

It could be argued that the preparation for fast swimming starts even before the starting gun is fired. First, put yourself on the starting block with your legs waist distance apart. Too often swimmers place their feet shoulder distance apart. This is a common mistake and means that your legs will not be streamlined enough to hit the water at the right angle.

What comes next

When you grip the edge of the diving platform, try not to grip too tightly. Too tight a grip means that you have to waste a fraction of a section undoing yourself from the platform, making it too tempting to spread your hands rather than cup them. Next, while you are getting ready to dive, make sure that you are bending slightly at the waist rather than hunching over.

Getting your focus right
Your focus should not be on the water immediately below you. It should be on the far end of the pool, because the objective of the dive is not to enter the water below, it is instead to make as much progress as quickly as possible to that far end of the pool. The purpose of this focus is not just psychological – looking into the distance will also ensure that your arms and neck adopt the right position when you push off.

On the starting gun
The important thing about your push off following the starting gun is that everything needs to be simultaneous. You need to use the power in your core, arms and legs at the same time for maximum effect. This is something that takes practice and co-ordination. Once again, it is also something that might benefit from being filmed, as it is difficult to judge for yourself "in the moment" whether each part of your body is acting in unison.

As you hit the water
As you hit the water, be sure to point your fingers and your toes, to make yourself as long as possible. The more streamlined you are, the quicker you will pass through the water.

Kick hard and fast

Once you are in the water, the next thing to do is kick as hard and as fast as possible. If you ever watch Olympic swimmers, you will have seen that they often do a dolphin kick (which involves both legs moving up and down together and is typically seen with the butterfly stroke). Start your first arm stroke as soon as possible, and resist the temptation to ride out the cruise you will get on the strength of the push off. This part of a dive is very similar to the last part of a flip turn, where you need to take action to capitalise on your strong push off as soon as possible rather than waiting for it to "run out" before you do anything else!

Chapter 9 - Outdoor swimming and open water swimming

Do men who have got all their marbles go swimming in lakes with their clothes on? P.G. Wodehouse

If you are taking part in a triathlon, you will probably have to complete the swimming leg of it outdoors in open water. Open water competitions and endurance events are not limited to the coast. They can involve swimming up large rivers in cities, or swimming between two points in lakes and canals.

Whilst this is the same sport that your indoor swimming cousins are practising, there is a slightly different slant on your training to swim fast. Accordingly, the following issues are pertinent to swimming fast outside:

Acclimatise gradually

Wherever in the world you live, the sea will be cooler than your local pool, so it is worth acclimatising over a period of time before the day of the triathlon or open water race. If you have plenty of time, start in the summer in a "shortie" wetsuit, and then gradually bulk up your swimming kit as the weather turns to autumn, when you will need a thicker suit with a swimming hat. Then when winter is over, you can get out your thinner gear again. Indoor swimmers can be surprised at the number of outfits that outdoor swimmers have to own, in order to be able to swim for all or most of the year.

The colder water may be a shock at first, so during your first couple of outdoor training sessions do not train hard. Twenty minutes of swimming at an easy pace is enough. The purpose of those initial two swims is to get you used to being in the open water. Do not beat yourself up if your speed is not what it is indoors.

Get into the right frame of mind for outdoor swimming

It is easy in a pool to mark off stages of your swim, whether you do this by counting lengths or by looking at the clock. In the sea it is difficult to keep an eye on the time, and it can be tricky to measure distances. You can counter this dragging feeling by being realistic about your goals, and by being positive about the swim.

Swim with safety in mind

Even in a pool with no lifeguard, there is usually someone around who would spot you if you were in trouble. This is obviously not the case with the sea, so take care that you train with someone else, and that you have support in place where appropriate.

Increasing your range gradually

On one hand, it is easy to swim further in the sea, because there is no one else that you need to avoid and your flow will not be broken by the sides of the pool requiring you to turn every so often. However, the effect of waves can be a surprisingly difficult force to work against, as the swimmer is thrown around in the sea. Get used to that feeling that you are not quite making the progress that you deserve.

The advantages of a bit of blubber

This is not an insult. Whales and seals have plenty of fat to keep them warm and assist their buoyancy, and the same can be said if you are an outdoor swimmer with a few pounds to spare. Call it insulation!

Are you afraid of fish?

Ichthyophobia is more common than you might think. In most cases, fear of fish is irrational, because the worst that can happen is that you have an unpleasant sensation as your foot brushes against one. However, jellyfish can give nasty stings, so wear a wetsuit and stay watchful in the water.

Think of the environment

In this context, thinking of the environment means considering the risk of hypothermia and acting on the warning signals. Your body will no doubt be

feeling colder than it would in a pool, but as soon
as breathing becomes harder than it should be or
you can feel that your circulation is not right,
attract the attention of the safety boat and get out
of the water.

Chapter 10 - Breathing and Swimming fast

There are so many things that a swimmer has to take into account when they are trying to swim fast. Technique, drag, core strength, but they most of all need to bear in mind their breathing rate and volume.

Training hard with your swimming is enough to improve your cardiovascular fitness, but you can also run and cycle to build up your efficiency. Running in particular can help you to develop your timing, as runners typically time their breaths in accordance with their steps. However, there are a few swimming specific tips that you can adopt that should improve your swimming performance.

Don't forget to breathe out!

Sometimes it can feel as though the focus on swimming breathing is all about the breathing in. In fact, when you think of a swimmer's breaths, you think of urgent gasps of air as they fill their lungs at every opportunity.

But swimmers neglect exhalation at their peril. Of course they breathe out, but they do not give the exhalation as much attention as the inhalation! Or they try to make their exhalation take place when they have a chance to inhale, which leads to shallow breathing.

The key to breathing well as a swimmer is to exhale into the water, and leave your dry moments free for inhalation. You may have a psychological barrier to breathing out in water because it feels strange. However, you need to get over this fast to swim fast!

In fact, for optimum speed you need to exhale constantly for all the time that you are not inhaling. This, rather than the pattern of in-hold-hold-out, is what will relax you into a loose enough style to get maximum velocity. So what you should be doing is breathing in-out-out-out-out-out. No holding allowed!

Try not to lift your head

In the chapter above about drag, we learnt that the raising your head can have the effect of lowering your feet and legs, which increases the resistance that you feel on the water and reduces your speed. Accordingly, if you turn your head to breathe rather than lift it, you can carry on stroking without your legs dropping, and therefore without affecting your rhythm or your drag.

If you keep your head down, you will create a pocket of air to your side. Instead, rotate your head to the side and breathe in that pocket. If you are not sure what this means, drag a football along in a similar position to your head. You will note that the ball has a little "bow wave" in front of it, which widens out into an arrowhead either side. The gaps between the sides of this arrowhead and your ball form the trough that is the perfect space for you to breathe in, as this is slightly lower than the rest of the water. Turning your head to breathe in the trough is much better than lifting your head up over its own "bow wave".

Do not rotate too far
Have you ever noticed that you are getting a stiff neck when you swim? If so, this could be as a result of rotating your head to the side too much. A new swimmer could be forgiven for thinking that they cannot win. On one hand they have only just learnt to rotate the head, and then they are told that they rotate their heads too much!

A simple way to gauge whether you are rotating your head too far is to see whether you are lifting both of your goggles out of the water at the same time. If you are, that is too far. You should only have one eye out of the water. In fact, the only part of you that needs to leave the water is your mouth.

Breathe bilaterally
Bilateral breathing simply means breathing on both sides, rather than favouring one side. Favouring one side is tempting, especially if you have one side of your body that is stronger than the other. For various reasons, most people have a dominant side due to injury or due to strengths honed in other sports you do which involve holding a racquet or club in the same hand all the time (like tennis or golf). Breathing on one side is also

tempting and somewhat habitual if you are a runner who cadences their breathing to fall on the same foot every time.

The dangers of breathing on one side are that you become lop sided and develop a habit of cross over, where the arm from your dominant side crosses over into the space of your weaker side. But there are other dangers to being a one-sided breather. This trait also interferes with getting a good rolling habit, which is important when you are trying to swim fast.

To ensure that you swop sides, why not cadence your breath so that you breathe on alternate strokes? For most swimmers, a ratio of 3 strokes is fine (breathe-stroke-stroke), but some swimmers choose to go for 5 of even 7 strokes.

If you find that this too unnatural and takes you away from the focus of getting up speed, you could even swim with your breathing on one side for one length, and swop for the journey back again. This has the advantage of not becoming too dependent on one side, but also of not adding the stress of switching sides during the same length if you are not used to it.

Keep your head still in between breaths

If you rotate your head constantly this is not only a waste of energy but can be exhausting and may lead to a neck injury. This is one of those habits that you may not even know that you have, so ask another swimmer to watch you while you are swimming so that they can let you know.

If you do habitually roll your head, one trick you could try to stop is to imagine there is a glass of water on top of your head that will spill if you move too much. Try to keep the glass level (in between breaths) during the course of the swim.

Chapter 11 - Is there any point in cross training?

If you want to get better at swimming, then the only training you should do is in the pool, right? Some swimmers do certainly believe this, and hold that they belong in the pool for every day of their training regime.

But this is rather a short sighted view. Cross training can be helpful for the following reasons:

- Cross training reduces boredom. If you are sick of going to the pool, you can maintain or improve your fitness levels by working out in the gym, getting on your bike or even by running. In fact, anything that gets your heart pumping can come in handy to improving your overall swimming ability because your aerobic capacity is an important factor in your success as a swimmer.

- Cross training can be fun! You are not being disloyal to swimming if you enjoy a dance class or get stuck into martial arts! As long as you are not sucked into another sport and diverting your training time away from swimming towards your new found obsession, enjoying other sports is not threat to your swimming training.

- You could learn something from other sports. For instance, runners find it easy to measure and control their breathing, which is certainly something that swimmers need to work on if they are going to improve their speed. Likewise, cyclists train for hours on end and may have tips to share on boosting your endurance.

- Swimming can sometimes be difficult to fit into your day. If you have a busy lifestyle, it can be tough to find time to go to the pool. But running or walking, for example, can start at the door (as opposed to having to drive to the pool and then get changed in the changing room). It is also worth going running or walking for just 15 minutes, if that is all the time you have. The chances are that you cannot even drive to the pool in 15 minutes!

What types of training can be helpful for swimmers?

Any other exercise is beneficial, but the following forms of exercise can be particularly helpful to swimmers.

Running

Running can be helpful for two reasons. Firstly, it is free and convenient. As set out above, you can set off at any time, and easily fit in a quick jog when you do not have time to swim. But it is also a good exercise in getting your breath to match your leg strokes. Elite runners cadence their breathing

74

so they breathing in for 2 steps and out for 2. For swimmers, controlling breathing is always a good idea. One small caveat: if your knees are weak, avoid running because it is high impact and could compound the problem.

Cycling
If you have difficulty with weight bearing exercise (which is why you might have chosen swimming in the first place), you could try cycling as an alternative to swimming. Cycling can build up your lower body strength, which is often neglected by swimmers because they are told so many statistics about how little propulsion comes from their legs. Cycling is also great for building your endurance, as the distances covered by cyclists mean that they can go for miles and miles in a single session.

Pilates
If you are the kind of person who thinks that training is just about thrashing hard in the pool, sweating buckets on the track or getting saddle sore on a bike, the power of something as gentle as Pilates may come as a pleasant surprise. This muscle conditioning set of exercises can improve tone and quality of the condition of your whole body. It is particularly good for core strength, which of course is essential to be a powerhouse in the swimming pool.

Dance

Dance? Yes you did read that correctly. Dancing can help co-ordination. Given that swimming is a whole body sport, dance can improve the speed with which your central nervous system connects with your muscles.

Football and other team games

The most important thing about these types of games is that you are enjoying physical activity, so you can include a couple of hours in your week without really "noticing" it. Games where you have to change direction quickly like football are helpful for keeping your reactions fast.

The gym

Some people find training in the gym a bit like being a hamster in a wheel. The repetitive nature of certain activities can quickly turn to boredom. For others, on the other hand, the gym is a welcome chance to build specific muscles groups. By focusing your effort on a particular part of your body, you can see quick results. You can also address any issues that you or your coach have raised, and fix them more quickly than if you were to try to do so in the pool.

How much cross training should your regime include?

If you are training for a triathlon, then no doubt your training schedule will effectively look like cross training anyway. But if you are a "pure" swimmer, how often should you get out of the pool and onto the track/gym/dance studio?

Bizarrely, the answer to this question depends on how you view the concept of rest. For some, rest days are sacred, so no sports equipment must be lifted and no sports kit can be worn. But for others, a day without any sport at all can be torture. If you fit into the latter category, then you should do Pilates or cycle on your rest days, to make sure that you get fix of exercise but still get your break from swimming but without pounding away at your body.

Cross training should be no more than 25% of your training regime, but no less than 10%. All work and no play makes Jack a dull swimmer!

The brick – swim/run

If you are new to swimming you may be surprised at how much terminology there is. A brick, in this case, refers to two disciplines of exercise that are joined together, usually two of the parts of a triathlon. For the most part, triathletes train using the running and cycling elements more often because they are both easy to manage and on dry land.

However, the swim/run needs to be done too, in order to make your transition easier when you are taking part in a real triathlon event. This transition is tricky if you do most of your training in a pool (as most people do), because the swimming pool owners quite rightly do not want people dripping past the reception desk in a swimming costume or wetsuit and stripping off in the car park. All the same, if the weather is suitable, why not factor in an outdoor swim/run brick session to your training regime? This will stand you in good stead for a triathlon, and even if you are not training for one, will certainly test your cardiovascular fitness and break the monotony of swimming lengths!

Chapter 12 - The importance of core strength to swimmers

To swimmers and many other sportsmen, the core muscles are unsung heroes. This is because they are unlikely to get injured, and are not prone to the repetitive injuries that are the danger of overuse sports. Core strength is essential for swimmers for two reasons:

First, having core stability means that you are at less risk from the imbalances felt by athletes which can lead to injury. In this context core means hips, abdominals and lower back muscles. Given that the parts of your body that you use to propel yourself forward in the water are all connected to these parts, core muscles that function well will help reduce the chances of getting an injury. This is particularly relevant to the shoulders where swimmers are concerned, as your shoulders tend to bear the brunt of the force that is created by the arms. So core strength for swimmers means injury protection for your shoulders.

Secondly, having a strong core means that your "star" muscles can perform to the best of their ability. Unless you are talking about a very small number of strength training exercises in the gym, no activity involves an isolated muscle group alone. They are all connected somehow. So a strong core means that the other parts of a swimmer's body can also function well.

Is gym work enough to build core strength?

Gym work is great for building core strength.
Common garden sit ups and donkey kicks can
help, as can machine work when it comes to hips
and lower back. Planking, the bridge and the
superman exercise (where you lay over an exercise
ball and adopt a flying posture – perhaps when the
gym is empty) are all helpful.

However, rather than just working out to get a six
pack, you need to extend your focus on core
strength for balance and agility, which means
stepping outside of the weights room. In fact, you
can significantly improve your core stability by
improving your posture alone.

If you have a desk job, which most people do, you
are at risk of poor posture as you slouch over a
desk or computer. Given that you sit down for
most of the day, you are at risk of that posture
becoming your permanent natural stance. So every
now and again throughout your working day, make
sure that you put your shoulders back and your
chest out, so that your back straightens and your
stomach muscles are encouraged to hold your back
in the right way.

How can you build up your core stability?

The following disciplines than can help build your
core strength seem rather gentle for an athlete who
is training hard, but are nevertheless important for
core muscle condition and posture. All three of
these disciplines do come with the warning that

poor technique can make your core weaker and cause injury, so it is essential to learn them under the tutelage of a properly qualified practitioner. It is no co-incidence that all three of these disciplines also make the swimmer slow down and become more mindful, which will help you to cope with the stress of a race situation and build your stamina generally.

Pilates

This discipline was started in the First World War by a German called Joseph Pilates. He was interned for some years and made use of this time by studying his breathing and core muscles and the effect various exercises had on them. When the First World War ended Pilates went to America, where he taught dancers who, being already aware of their bodies immediately caught on to the benefits of the exercise. But it was not until the exercise spread in the 1980s that Pilates became widely available.

Alexander Technique

Over 100 years old, the Alexander Technique makes you redirect your mind and body to use your muscles more effectively. It focuses on the efficiency with which you use your body, especially in relation to your head and neck. Through the various exercises and techniques, the practitioner becomes more mindful, and more confident about their body's abilities.

Yoga

The origins of yoga can be traced back to India, and versions of it exist in the Hindu and Sikh traditions. There are various forms of yoga, but the most common in the West is hatha yoga, which is based around a number of postures. The focus of yoga is mindfulness, so whilst the practitioner Is considering their muscles and the way in which they can be stretched and moved, there is also a focus on spirituality.

Whoever would have guessed that you started out building your core strength for swimming training and ended up finding spiritual enlightenment?

Chapter 13 - Nutrition and swimming

If you think about it, what you put into your body to fuel it is as important as the training techniques you use. So if you are serious about learning to swim faster, there is no point undoing all of the hard work that you have put into your training by eating junk food.

How many calories do you need each day? Women are advised not to exceed 2,000 calories, and men 2,500. However, someone who is training hard is advised to consume much more than that. In fact, Michael Phelps who won numerous gold medals in the 2008 Beijing Olympics was reputed to eat up to 10,000 calories per day, claiming that all he could do was "eat, sleep and swim."

That is of course excessive and perhaps unachievable for the average part time sportsman, but closer to 3,000 calories is probably more appropriate for someone who is training hard.

Where do you get your fuel from?

Swimming hard and fast rapidly depletes the glycogen that you store in your muscles. When your energy runs out, you will not be able to carry on swimming – at least not at your previous pace. Glycogen is how your body stores energy and is typically from carbohydrate. So carbohydrate is needed for energy levels to be re-stocked.

Are all carbs created equal?

If you are a devotee of the Atkins diet, or its more recent competitor the Dukan diet, you will have been conditioned into the mindset that carbs are bad. Indeed, both of these diets aim to eradicate carbs from the plate of the dieter for at least most of the week.

Even if your motivation for learning to swim fast is to lose weight rather than to build cardiovascular endurance, cutting out carbs is not the way to achieve this, and you will need to re-educate your taste buds to overcome your aversion to them.

But all carbs are not created equal. Generally speaking, white carbs are bad, and wholemeal good. This is because the processing required to produce white versions of rice, flour and pasta remove some of the fibre in the food. Your body does not have to work so hard to get to the nutrients. With whole grains, the whole of the goodness is preserved.

How much of your diet should be carbohydrates?

As with any active person, carbs should make up around 70% of your diet. This can include:

- Wholemeal bread
- Wholemeal pasta
- Brown rice
- Bananas
- Fruits

Your breakfast should be an opportunity to eat plenty of carbs to give yourself optimum energy for the day ahead. Your snacks during the day should include small portions of carbs that are easy to digest, and are not refined (e.g. bleached flour or processed meals).

The importance of protein in your quest to swim fast

If carbs are the fuel that will get you swimming fast, then protein is the building block. So you need to supplement your wholegrain carbs with a fair amount of protein, which should make up around 20% of your diet.

Some swimmers think that their new found love of the sport is an excuse to eat all the junk food and fat that they want. Whilst being well padded can help keep you warm on sea swims, swimming is not a licence to eat fatty foods.

Protein not only helps to grow healthy muscle, but it also promotes the healing process where you have been injured. Accordingly, by choosing lean proteins, you can keep yourself strong and injury resistant. Lean proteins include fish, lean red meat, chicken, shell food and game.

The importance of fats

Bad fat (that is solid at room temperature) is not good for the heart. Saturated fats and trans fats can clog your arteries and cause serious health problems. But there are good fats that are not only helpful for the absorption of soluble minerals, but they are also valuable in their own right. Confused about the difference between "good" and "bad" fats?

Fish oils and other sources of omega 3 are helpful sources of good fats, and are useful for joints (as well as eye and brain health). Although swimming is not a weight bearing sport, it can be tough on your joints. The frog kick that goes with breaststroke can be tough on your knees, and all styles are tough on your shoulders.

Foods containing the healthy (monounsaturated and polyunsaturated) fats that should be included in your diet include seeds, nuts, oily fish, olive oil, peanut oil, and avocadoes.

How can you change your diet without too much pain?

The trouble with cutting down on fats is that the convenient foods are often those that are the worst for you. Commercially based goods in particular are notorious for piling on the pounds. But you do not have to become a martyr to your food. You can enjoy different versions of your favourite dishes, slightly amended to improve their fat profile. Instead of butter, choose an olive oil spread. For red meats, substitute chicken or fish.

Vitamins and minerals

Most people can get all of the vitamins and minerals they need to be healthy (and be a fast swimmer) from a balanced diet. However, some people do believe that taking a multivitamin will give them a boost. Please consult your medical professional before taking any supplement. Vitamins have many different uses, but most importantly for swimmers are the vitamins that help promote a strong immune system and encourage the healthy development and operation of a strong blood stream.

Minerals like calcium are particularly important for strong bones, and magnesium and iron for healthy blood.

Before the swim

What should you eat immediately before the swim? Foods that give you energy, but that are easily digested. So wholegrain cereals are ideal, particularly if you are staying in a hotel where there is a breakfast bar with plenty of choice.

If you are looking for something that is easier to transport, why not go for a sandwich made with wholegrain bread? A banana sandwich is idea because its sweetness makes it easy to eat – particularly if you are nervous before a triathlon.

After the race

After the race is over, it can be tempting to get so caught up in how well or badly you have swum to forget about refuelling. But eating after you exercise is an important part of the recovery process. One of the easiest ways to do this is to drink fresh fruit juice, so that you can swig it in little gulps and still get caught up in the whole post swim discussions. After a very long swim, do not forget to drink some electrolytes as your glycogen stores will be very depleted.

Drinking or eating after the intense exercise is very important. If you think that your freshly squeezed orange juice is too acidic tasting, why not try diluting the juice with water?

Water, water everywhere but no a drop to drink?

You may not realise it when you are swimming, thanks to the cool water. But there is a danger of dehydration. The worst case scenario is that you become very ill and dry. However, the kind of dehydration that leaves you feeling slightly exhausted is still bad for you, and can be avoided by keeping your fluid level up.

Why not bear the following things in mind for hydration:

- Drink little and often, when you have a chance;
- If you find water boring, choose another liquid. It does not matter what you choose, just as long as it is wet!;
- If you can get another food group into the liquid (e.g. orange juice) so much the better;
- Do not take long glugs infrequently;

- If there is no water provided at the venue, get a strategically placed friend to hand you everything you need.

Chapter 14 - Wearing the right kit

I simply can't understand
Why swimsuits are in such demand
They're soggy and damp,
Bind like a clamp,
And hold about three pounds of sand!
D.R. Benson

No doubt that every swimmer has felt like this at some point in his or her career. But now, the options available are so technologically advanced that it almost feels as though you need a PhD in Physics to choose the right one. Where do you start?

We have seen from the chapter above that there are many techniques that have been tried to reduce the amount of drag swimmers face. It is a constant battle during all stages of the swim, whether the swimmer is diving, streamlining, pulling, catching, rotating and even breathing.

So if you have put all of that effort into the goal of reducing drag, you need to carry the project through to include paying attention to what you wear. If clothes maketh man, can a swimsuit maketh a swimmer?

Swimming caps are commonplace, and cover the swimmer's hair with material to make the surface of the head smoother and providing a better drag profile.

When Speedo brought out their fastskins, there was much pomp and ceremony because the company believed that it had mimicked sharkskin and harnessed the secrets of fish for human swimmers to enjoy. By making fastskins with V shaped ridges in them, the surface of the suits resembled sharkskin, which meant that the water in the pool flowing around a swimmer would be directed more efficiently.

The science behind these V shaped ridges is that they aggravate the water and creates turbulence around the suit. This means that there is a balance between levels of water flow. The question is, does it work? It is difficult to measure how fast someone would have swum in one set of conditions, and then, in a completely separate race, use that as a test case.

Speedo had claimed that the suits would make drag resistance so easy that the suits would save up to 7.5% in efficiency. Many people must have thought that they were buying something special, turning up to championships with the expectation that they could outswim Jaws. However, a study carried out by the publications Sports Biomechanics claimed the benefit bestowed by the fast suits was only a more modest 2%.

Were the suits a waste of time? It is difficult to say. If you are an elite professional swimmer, then surely a difference of 2% could be the difference between a medal and no medal, or even the difference between colours of medals.

For an enthusiastic amateur, you could say that the suit might give you the psychological advantage, believing that you could beat anyone. This is harmless. However, you might have to contend with other swimmers wanting to get up close and have a look at the suit.

A close shave?

A move that you could take that may be a lot cheaper than getting a swimming suit designed by scientists is to shave. The whole of the body can be shaved to improve swimming performance. Scientists have shown that the effects of this on your times can be profound, as there is less friction drag. Shaving your body hair is probably one of the cheapest things that a swimmer can do to improve their resistance in the water. When you consider that all it takes is a few moments extra in the shower and that it is almost as effective as high performance suits, shaving is probably one of the best things that you can do with your time from the point of view of efficiency!

It is often said that water is 1,000 times more viscous than air, although this number does vary between scientists. Taking this into account, there are three different types of drag that a swimmer's body must try to combat. Firstly, there is frictional drag. This involves the swimmer's body's and how it interacts with the water molecules in the swimming pool, which end up slowing you down. But somewhat counter-intuitively, the same force enables your propulsion. That is because that same force resists against your hands when you are pressing back, and your feet when you are kicking. The faster you get, the more frictional drag is an issue. But what about lift? This is what determines your horizontal position in the water. There is an interplay between the forces that govern your body going forwards or backwards (drag) and those going up and down (lift).

If you were designing a life jacket, lift would be the first thing on your mind, rather than drag. So the most important issue would be how to keep the swimmer afloat. When looking at kit for swimming races and swimming fast, it is assumed that the swimmer keeps himself afloat and that the most important thing is to give that swimmer speed.

How can a suit give you speed? This is an interesting question, because in competitive swimming, not only do you want to increase speed, you also need a way of swimming faster that does not involve expending much more energy, because this would be unsustainable. FINA is the international body that governs swimming and decides which suits should be allowed in competitions. For triathlons, you are typically told to wear the wetsuit that is most appropriate to the weather conditions.

A suit that has not really been matched in terms of drag reduction is the LZR racer, which has received the FINA approval and was used in the

2008 and 2012 Olympic Games. LZR is reputed to make enormous differences to performance. Not only is the material that they are made out of a quarter of the length of regular swimsuit material, it is also flatter and smoother than shaven skin. Being water resistant, the suits do not absorb water. So there is no compromise on the swimmer's buoyancy. The swimmer does not have to pay the price of this suit by having to deal with a garment that is waterlogged.

Speedo have also revolutionised the way in which they manufacture these suits, because their factories have done away with seams. Instead, the pieces are welded together.

Can Speedo improve on the design of swimmers themselves? It is true that not only is the material of the LZR outstanding at sliding through the water, the suit tries to perfect's its owner's faults too.

People are not a streamlined shaped. Even the most toned of swimmers will have inconvenient lumps and bumps detracting from the torpedo shape that would have been the ideal form to take when moving through the water. So the suit has panels that aim to smooth out the swimmer's lumps and bumps and make them into a better shape for fighting drag.

But as if it was not enough that your swimsuit is accusing you of having lumps and bumps where they should not be, the LZR also comes with a core stabiliser. This is essentially a girdle made of double thickness material. The core stabiliser encourages swimmers to find their balance and engage their abdominal muscles when they are on endurance swims. It is not clear what method is used for this, but it is thought that the pressure the suit exerts is enough to make you want to move into a more efficient position. Speedo have said that the suit has been tested thoroughly and there has never been any problem experiencing restricted breathing as a result of the tightness of these suits.

What else do you need?

Aside from a swimsuit, there is nothing really that a swimmer needs, but there may be a number of things that may help them when training to swim fast.

Pull paddles

Pull paddles divide opinion in the racing fraternity. The macho approach is that they are great. The bigger the better. These paddles come in a range of shapes and sizes, which means that there is a wide variety to choose from. At first glance, they look a little like rigid oven gloves.

The swimmer pulls them through the water, and the paddles collect more than the swimmer's hand would have done. In the same way that a cyclist takes off bike weights and finds that the course is in fact far easier than he had thought, a swimmer can remove their paddles after training and find that the race is much easier than they thought. /One downside of these is that they do force swimmers to pull much harder than usual. This makes the swimmer vulnerable to injury, if they do not warm up adequately and if they push themselves too hard.⟩

But like anything, this is a personal choice. Pull paddles are relatively inexpensive and may be worth a try. Why not ask someone you see has they at the pool whether you can have a go?

Pull buoys

There are floats that go between your legs to keep you from sinking while you are doing drills that focus on your arms, head and neck.

Underwater camera

It may be a real luxury to own one, but you may be able to borrow one from time to time to check on your own style. Work with a partner on this one, and video each other. It is all very well to describe to someone what they are doing wrong, but so much easier to show them. Any why focus on the negatives? Perhaps you have better get hold of a camera to find out what you are doing right!

Goggles

Given the advice in this book about your head being best in the water at all time, goggles are a must. If you intend to spend some serious hours in the gym in the next few months, it is worth spending some money on some good quality ones. You will find that the different manufacturers all have their own quirks. Check that the goggles are the right shape for your head (e.g. oval or round etc). if these goggles are going to be protecting your eyes for the next couple of years, they had better fit straight.

Flippers

With new strokes or where you are concentrating on your arms, it can be helpful to wear flippers to take the pressure off your legs and give them a bit of a boost. However, some swimmers are critical of using flippers because they do not think that the scenario should change between the training session and the race (where flippers are not allowed).

A good timepiece

Most decent sized swimming pools have a large clock on the wall. However, it you can afford it, you may wish to look into the idea of getting a watch with a timer on it. Not only could you easily time yourself, but the computer chip would be able to store the information about your previous swims, so that you would have your information to hand.

Waterproof MP3 player

Did you know that such things exist? They do and they could alleviate the boredom that sometimes settles in on long training sessions.

Nose clip

This may not be the most expensive bit of swimming kit you own, but it may be the one that changes your life. You will have read above that the key to breathing technique is to breathe out constantly. In swimming, you should breathe in and out through your mouth. Once you have got used to the sensation of wearing a nose clip, it is reassuring to know that you can do a flip turn, dive, or even just cadence your breathing without the water disappearing up your nose!

Chapter 15 - Developing the mental toughness needed to swim fast

As with all sports, it is not enough to be strong physically. You have to be strong mentally to get the most out of your body. This chapter deals with how to approach your training generally, and then goes on to discuss how to approach the day of the race itself.

Generally

What are your goals for swimming fast? Do you want to be an Olympic champion, win a 400m race at your local pool or somewhere in between?

Clear and realistic goal setting

If you have had an appraisal in the workplace in the last 10 years, you will probably have been asked to set SMART goals for yourself. SMART is an acronym which stands for Specific, Measurable, Attainable, Realistic and Timely. The formula is well known in the business world, but can also be used in the sporting sphere, to make sure that athletes and would be athletes have to stretch themselves, but within sensible boundaries.

Why not study the times of others who have completed the distance you are targeting, and come up with a goal time for yourself? World records are set out above. If you are a beginner to the sport, you may wish to make your goal stepped, so that you have a number of miniature goals to achieve on your way to the Big One. This means that you will not be disheartened by the length of time it takes for you to get there.

Of course, if you have entered a triathlon then the goal has already been set for you (usually 1 mile for swimming), so why not break that down into smaller chunks of outdoor swimming until you get to whole mile in a respectable time?

Making a commitment

How serious are you about reaching your swimming goals? To make decent progress, you need to train regularly, rather than letting a written plan of swimming goals fade in your notebook without being referred to.

Be realistic about the time you have available. If you work a 60 hour week and have a young family, you will not be able to train for an hour a day. But two half hour sessions might be doable. Joining a swimming club can be a good way to make sure that you turn up when your schedule tells you that you should. Most decent people are more likely to turn up so they don't let the club down!

Some swimmers find that their commitment increases if they hold themselves to account about the regime. So if you start a blog, for example, you may not get many readers. But there is always the theoretical possibility that you are letting your readers down or not delivering on what you promised was going to happen.

Affirmations

Affirmations can sound a bit "New Age" if you are not used to the idea. But repeating motivating phrases to yourself as you swim lap after lap can help you to reinforce your self-confidence. If you are new to swimming and have just tried the sport after some successes in cycling and running, you might find it frustrating that you are moving so slowly after the speeds you have reached in those other disciplines.

Affirmations you may like to try during your swimming training include: I am strong, I am fast, I can reach the end of this lap.

Visualisation

Visualisation can be powerful in motivating swimmers, because it commands another sense to take part in fulfilling your ambitions. By "seeing" yourself on the podium, or successfully completing the swim section of a triathlon, you are one step closer to achieving that goal.

Training with other people before the race day

If you are the kind of person who likes to train on their own, that is fine. But you need to race against other people before the day of the race in order to get used to the feeling of having others alongside you.

For this reason alone, it is worth joining a club so that you can use friendly races to prepare you for the big day.

On the day itself

Now we turn to tricks that you can do on the day itself, to keep your focus and get the best out of all the training you have put in.

Dealing with nerves – letting the stroke rhythm take you over

Some swimmers get so nervous that they throw up before the race starts. They get so wound up with tension, their stress takes over their whole body, including their digestive system. It is true that the moments before the race can be very tense. However, the process of swimming can be very soothing, if you allow it to be. The one two one two of stroking can settle your nerves. So instead of dreading the moment that you have to get into the pool, actively look forward to it, as a welcome way to soothe your nerves.

Perhaps the worst moments for nerves are the couple of minutes before you get onto the block. You may have done some breathing exercises in the changing room, and listened to relaxing music in the car on the way to the pool, but how can you control the adrenalin flowing as you walk up the side of the pool towards your block?

104

A certain amount of nervous energy is a good thing. It should set your performance apart from a training swim, and spur you on to swim your best. So firstly, do not let your perfectly respectable pre-race apprehension mushroom into an all-consuming panic. Instead, acknowledge the nerves and meet them head on with steady breathing. If you need to, mentally tell yourself "I am nervous, but I am in control."

Keep your eye on your own lane

Everyone checks out the competition before and during the race. It's just human nature. In fact, it can be very helpful to look at other swimmers before the race and reflect on what they are doing right, and what they are doing wrong. Is their catch and pull technique perfect? Do they have a funny way of kicking?

It can also be motivating in a good way to have others in the pool to pace yourself with. Being part of the crowd in a triathlon can spur you on, when you would otherwise be splashing about at sea. However, for some swimmers, concentrating on what their opponents are up to is a significant distraction from their own performance. The distraction can either come from nerves, when you sense that another swimmer is much better than you and lose hope; or it can come from a loss of focus. You are meant to be giving your attention to what is happening in your own lane, not everyone else's!

What can you do about it? The simple answer is to stay vigilant to the danger of gazing too much to either side to see what your competitors are up to. If you do find yourself mentally drifting into the next lane, draw your focus back gently and carry on.

Think of now, not later or before
Depending on the race, you could have a lot riding on this particular swim, even if is "just" your self-esteem rather than money. Perhaps this race is the determining moment of a tournament. Maybe you are being watched by someone who is important to you. Or you may even be in the running for a prize sum.

For some swimmers, the distraction is not thoughts of the future but memories or reflections about the past. If you have had a bad experience in that particular pool, it might put you off. On the other hand, if you have had a previous triumph there, you might be swimming under a false sense of security.

It is all too easy when you are in the race to think about yourself on the podium, or worry about not being on the podium. Whilst visualisation techniques can be helpful generally in your training, the race itself should be all about now. If you do find your attention travelling to the past or the future, make sure that you bring your focus back to the stroke in hand. It is too much to think that you should focus only on one stroke at a time. Instead, have a plan for the overall race, but take it one lap at a time.

Chapter 16 - Swimming injuries and how to avoid them

Swimming injuries? Are you surprised to know they exist? Whilst it is true that swimming is a low impact sport, it is possible to injure yourself due to poor technique, overuse, or simply overdoing it. Some swimmers may have a biomechanical fault, which means that they joints or bones may be misaligned. If you keep getting an injury that either becomes very painful very suddenly or one that keeps recurring when you do not think that you are pushing yourself too hard, do not panic. Take yourself to a sports physiotherapist. It is worth paying to see one, because they will appreciate that your injury has been caused by a sport. In particular, try to find a sports physio who enjoys swimming and knows exactly what you are talking about.

Swimmers shoulder

There are a number of injuries to the shoulder that are caused by swimming. Some are sharp pains, others dull aches, or tears to tendons.

How are shoulder injuries caused by swimming? One common culprit is "crossing over" which means that your arms move diagonally during the catch and pull stage of the stroke, and stray over an imaginary axis extends above your head. If you have got into this habit, it can be quite difficult to break. Try asking someone else to watch you, head on, and comment on whether your arms are crossing over.

Lack of variety is also a problem. If you do the same style, day in day out, your body can simply get worn out. Given that your shoulder has a high workload when you swim, your shoulder is bound to suffer. Try different strokes in your training, to give your shoulder a break.

Some swimmers find that swim paddles (which help swimmers catch more water) can increase the resistance that they need to move through the water so much that their joints come under an unacceptable amount of pressure, and that they cause injuries. Accordingly, you could drop paddles completely from your training, or switch to alternative or smaller designs.

Finally, the cause of your "swimmers shoulder" could simply be that you have upped your training too much too soon whether in terms of distance or intensity. The answer there of course is that you need to slow down or take a break.

Whatever the cause of your swimmers shoulder is, tweaks that you can make to your technique to prevent its recurrence include making sure that you are breathing bilaterally (to make sure that both sides of your body are taking equal strain), and bending your elbow during the recovery phase of the stroke.

Knee injury

The trouble with the kick associated with the breast stroke is that it requires the leg to move in a way that is not compatible with the way in which your knee was designed to move. So whilst your freestyle kick involves an up and down motion, a breast stroke kick requires a frog like kick which makes your knee roll outwards. This rolling does not just affect the knee. All of the tendons and ligaments in your leg are affected, and sometimes swimmers can suffer from a wearing away of the cartilage under their knee.

To combat this, or to prevent it from happening, you need to do strengthening exercises (in the gym or just on dry land) to prepare your knees for this pressure. As you learned from the information about propulsion above, your legs only provide 10% of the force that propels your body forward. So it is easy to think that your legs are less important and do not deserve much attention when you are strength training. But this is a short sighted approach.

You also need to make sure that you warm up and cool down adequately, to make sure that your body is receptive to the activity.

Lower back injuries

Lower back injuries are often due to poor kicking technique, rather than arm activity. If you are finding it difficult to keep your body horizontal and float yourself in the water, try some drill exercises involving kicking while holding a float in your hands, to concentrate your efforts on your legs.

Neck injuries

We learned above that rotating your neck too much to breathe is bad for your technique and speed, because it can slow your stroke rhythm down and cause drag. But a more pressing reason to keep your head aligned with your spine is that head rotation brings a risk of neck injury.

Likewise, it is important to keep your head down (aside from taking breaths) for drag reduction purposes, but avoiding lifting your head is also helpful for avoiding drag.

Diving is inherently dangerous is you are not familiar with the area, and if the pool is too shallow. Accordingly, obey signs where they are displayed about the dangers in the area.

Finally, if you are doing backstroke, take care to find other ways of working out how far you are away from the edge of the pool, so that you can limit the number of times that you turn around to look for the edge.

Conclusion

In this book we have looked at the techniques and factors that explain why people are fast swimmers, and described some drills that you could use to achieve fast times.

The book contains details of how to improve your speed using various strokes, but the reality is that freestyle is the most prevalent in clubs and competitions so the chances are that you would be doing this. However, after reading the chapter on butterfly stroke, perhaps you might be tempted to give it a little go if there is no one else around at the pool!

Strength is important for swimming fast, but much more so is technique. For that reason, everyone, no matter what their level of competence or mobility is can apply the drills set out and see some kind of improvement.

If you are a triathlete, it may be a bit of a relief for the exercise to be all about the arms for once. And it may also be reassuring that, whilst in pictures of the swimming legs of triathlons it looks like a free for all, there are some techniques that you can take from this book to improve your mile time, which will of course improve your overall triathlon time.

Good nutrition is essential, and the very brief guide to the kind of diet you should be aiming for here could be a springboard for you or for your child to take some responsibility for their own diet.

Indeed, by learning what foods are best for swimming performance, a swimming mad child might set down some healthy eating habits that will stay with him or her for life.

If you have not yet joined a swimming club because you have not yet got around to it or felt embarrassed about the level of your swimming, move this up your list of priorities. Swimmers are generally a smiley and talkative bunch, and you may find your local swimming club an endless source of help and supportive advice. Even Michael Phelps turned up as the new boy once!

"It's a good idea to begin at the bottom in everything except in learning to swim." Anon

Made in United States
Troutdale, OR
01/30/2024

17305692R00066